The Covert Narcissist

By Audrey Davies

DEDICATION

This book is dedicated to my three children, my mother and father.

CONTENTS

ACKNOWLEDGMENTS

To all of the students on my psychotherapy course and my lecturers for helping me develop self-awareness, to protect myself from this type of abuse in the future and to help others. This book has been inspired by those who experience enormous pain, but are still able to show forgiveness, compassion and kindness.

1 SHOCK

Anger, confusion, misery, turmoil. Two years of therapy and two years of reading and an emotional dirge, a swamp. But then I had real clarity and relief.

This book is all about life with a narcissist. When I heard the word narcissist in the past I would think of someone famous, ostentatious, wrapped up in themselves, loud and brash. A look at me type of person, who everyone avoids, laughs at and enjoys. This narcissist, my narcissist was nothing like that.

My narcissist was my husband and he was a covert narcissist. There was not a lot of useful literature out there on this particular breed of narc, so here I write the book to tell you about mine.

I have read a lot about narcissistic abuse, books, blogs, youtube vlogs, experienced psychiatrists, doctors with PHD's, women and men who have got out of abusive relationships after 20 years of marriage, amateur life coaches with a large online following, it's a hot topic. So there must be a reason for that - every single person on the planet, will know one and at some point will have been intimate with one. They may not know it yet, but once they do, it's like your mind opens up to the truth, you enter another portal. It is a new way of seeing people and understanding them, especially those people in your life that just don't seem to make sense. When you read about and truly understand narcissism, things then really do start to make sense. Before you have this knowledge, these people are frustrating, puzzling, illogical, they can be relentlessly cruel and cold, at times entertaining and the closer they are to you, i.e. a boss or boyfriend, spouse then you need some armour, you need to be prepared and aware.

Before you learn about NPD you could just find these people odd, very charming one minute and then cruel the next - it's only usually when you get close to them, when you need them in some way that you start to experience the madness. They can get angry when you voice an opinion, always thinking they know best. But the damage and abuse they cause can be colossal; the slow and insidious abuse that can happen silently over decades can erode one's sense of self, making that individual feel like they actually no longer exist. You become a walking shell and that is what nearly happened to me. I say nearly, because I learnt the tools to break free.

Their voice and self seems so strong, so certain, and if you are the type to question yourself, then you are at greater risk. If someone says they are right, over and over again and they say you are wrong with such certainty, then you may start to believe it. It's how strong your sense of self is, that indicates the level by which you can get sucked into a narcissists web of annihilation.

It is how strong you own gut instinct is, and strength in knowing what is ok and what is not ok, that can determine whether you survive the narcissist or not.

Some physically abuse, destroy the physical body in some way, others try and destroy your soul, strength and character. I had the latter.

I was abused, but not psychically. I had something so disturbing, so silent, so gradual that it was much more dangerous, because no one else saw it and then no one else could help. All abuse is about power and control, the person who feels powerless (the narcissist), can then feel powerful.

So for the type of narcissistic abuse I suffered, it was all about how to bring someone down, without being overt about it. This is bringing someone down by being covert about it. Where no one else sees, and even you start to doubt it too.

For me, I didn't know it at the time, but it was like being in a room where the oxygen is very slowly taken away, so that you barely notice it until you are dead. The same with a frog, in a pot of water where the temperature rises very slowly - so the frog does not notice, then all of a sudden the water boils and the frog is dead.

What kills the frog is not the heat of the water, but not knowing when to jump out. I didn't jump out quickly enough.

At the end of my ordeal I felt like my spirit was dead, that nothing really gave me joy anymore. That I was walking around alive, but dead inside.

The domestic abuse I suffered was not an attack on the body, no bruises, breaks or cuts on the outside. They were all inside, and I have suffered greatly. But it took me a long time to see what was going on.

Abuse can be overt or covert. You can be shouted, hit and screamed at. You can be drip fed insidious lies over many years about how you are always wrong and everything you do is wrong, and that can slowly erode your sense of self or at least the person you used to be. You lose the strength to get away, because you lose the ability to trust your own judgement.

I say "I am proud", the narcissist would say, I had not done anything special. I say "I like", the other person says there is nothing to like, and why would I even suggest there was. Everything you like, everything you are proud of, everything you feel, everything you see, every opinion, every part of who you are they disagree with. It's so slight and subtle. That you are dead or nearly dead as in my case, before you have even noticed what is happening to you.

You try to please them and it is never enough. You say sorry to try and repair the situation even though you don't feel you have actually done anything wrong. Then you descend into a blur about what is actually right and wrong, you stop knowing what is right and wrong, your vision then becomes blurred in a mist of confusion. The uncertainty in yourself in your own decisions in what is right and wrong grows, so you are then at risk of more abuse.

So why did I put up with all of this? That is something only someone who has been through this will know. Is it because you witnessed this relationship growing up, you are a tolerant empath who always sees the good in people. You have low self esteem, and low self worth? You don't really know your own mind? You are always asking other people for advice, you lack a connection with yourself and your own certainty of what is right and wrong.

Perhaps as a child, your parent or parents made all the decisions and didn't allow you to grow and make choices as an autonomous free individual? They took too much control in your life. Perhaps you have a need to rescue people that seem lost and need your help. You could be an optimist always thinking things will get better. You could have low self worth and low expectations and think this is just life, and you have to put up with it.

You do not challenge or question a relationship that mirrors the one you experienced as a child. Your role models, i.e. your parents had a similar relationship so you don't expect or crave for anything better than what you witnessed for years growing up. Or if you have children you tolerate it, because you think everyone else is in the same boat.

Well all of the above reasons did apply to me, but something that I want to write about that has been overlooked I think a lot, is that we tolerate it, because we remember the person they were before.

There are three stages to a relationship with a narcissists, idealize, devalue and discard. You remember what they were like in the idealization phase. This can be a long period, a two year courtship in my case. Others it can be 10 years, 3 months, 6 years. Any period, where you fall in love, you base your opinion on the person they are at the beginning. We all do this, it's common sense. You have a period of courtship, then you make a commitment.

And this is the important bit, a transitional period which usually comes after a commitment of some type. You notice suddenly things are not quite the same, they withdraw, they are moody. Everything you do is wrong. It always happens at a point where you are in some way tied to them. That could be buying a house, having a baby, getting married. Where they think you are committed and need them and you are enmeshed in a way. They know that this is when you are less likely to leave, and they can sense that.

What is harder to spot is that a narcissist in the idealize phase (often just the first 2/3 months), will be unbelievably charming and vulnerable. It is a dangerous combination. Where you are charmed and showered with gifts and made to feel like the most beautiful person in the world, "the one". This bliss, often an intoxicating and euphoric feeling is very hard to forget.

What then becomes so baffling and so disturbing is how that wonderful incredible person who was perfect in every way, turns into a soulless monster.

Intoxicating is the right word, because it goes from intoxicating to toxic.

Many mental health professionals talk about narcissists like they are separate from us, the aliens among us. It's almost like you cut their arm and blood doesn't come out. The dead among us, the lifeless and dark, who look like us and sound like us, but are without the same level of empathy and conscience as the rest of us. "The empty ones" living in a shell of a body.

Some say for these people you cannot have hope in, you cannot hope they will change and you cannot hate them. If you do either of these two things, you will be destroyed.

To hope in them, is in a wasted belief that you can convince or reason with someone who has limited empathy.

Why would they suddenly care, why would they suddenly feel remorse. And the advice often is that it is **our** weakness to see the best in everyone sometimes. That we will only be pulled into the darkness if we stay and fight.

To hate is to be stuck in a bitter dark place where you wait for an apology that never comes.

I have heard the story of Myra Hindley or Rose West in prison, when they are asked to reveal if they killed any more victims and if so, where they are buried to help the families move on. I used to wonder, and I was shocked, appalled and confused when they refused to say. I thought these people are now locked up in prison for the rest of their lives - what does it mean to them to tell us. Why can't they reveal these details that would mean so much to the victims' families and friends. These people are being tortured daily as if they were dead themselves having to live with not knowing, waiting, wanting, hoping, praying for these serial killers to give them that tiniest bit of light, that glimmer of information that would end their terrible suffering and bring closure. But alas they won't get it, will they.

Ian Brady is now dead, and he didn't reveal the details of where his last victim Keith Bennett might be buried. He was given every opportunity in the last few hours of his life but he didn't divulge anything.

Someone who tortures and kills, innocent and vulnerable women or children, has no conscience. They have no empathy. They enjoy not telling people, they get a kick from suffering. For these people there is no hope. They only know control and power and they enjoy that from their prison cell.

But there is a spectrum of narcissists/psychopaths the ones without empathy the ones who can NEVER put themselves in another person's shoes. What these people share is a lack of empathy. But what makes them so much harder to spot is that they may be very convincing at showing it – a charm/manipulation. They know what it is, so can fake it when necessary, but they don't intrinsically have it. They show it in the idealisation phase, to get you hooked. Often mirroring your own behaviour and actions, values, standards and likes and dislikes. But once commitment/marriage/children, something where you are tied to them takes place, the erosion of self begins. So very slowly...They call it a drip drip effect.

There are milder versions and there are extreme cases. A boss that is never pleased with anything you do, who disagrees with everything you say, who gets a kick out of making people feel small and useless.

I remember a colleague of mine, who had multiple affairs. She would insult people and their looks in a way that almost seemed like she was complimenting them. Hugely charming to those who allowed her to get to the top of her chosen career, but inside you could see she was empty. There was nothing there.

Do I hate them? Yes some days I do. But the key to all hate, anger and suffering is to try your best to see things from the other persons side. Putting yourself in their shoes, something the narcissist cannot do, this is empathy. I believe with some narcissists to hope they will change is futile (although I will discuss this later in the book). But to feel an overwhelming intense every day anger and hatred will only rot you inside. To understand these people, you need to understand the root of where it comes from. In my experience understanding comes first, forgiveness follows. But there will be days where you hate, and there will be days where you feel deep sorrow for them and the misery they have suffered.

But there is one thing I can absolutely say without a shadow of a doubt, don't think you can change someone without empathy. Only they can change themselves, and if their abuse happened at a young age and lasted a long time I would say that the chances are slim. They can't remember a different life, so how can they then long for that life? A life they never knew. Where they were held and loved and adored by their mother or father. A place where love felt safe and secure and was given unconditionally.

That makes sense to me. If life has always been empty, if love has never been readily available, how can it then be something they desire. If for many years, those important 0-5 years were empty of real attachment and unconditional love, how can they then yearn for it. If empathy was not shown to them, how can they ever really know it and show it to others?

When my husband as a child hurt himself, his mother did not comfort him. She provided food, warmth, shelter and clean clothes, but there was no nurturing and emotional care. So how would he then be able to show it to

2 HOPE

This is a short chapter, but a very important one, and it is about hope.When do you give up on hoping the one you love will change.

I know many people reading this book will be able to identify with this.

If you take vows in church for example or a registry office in front of your family - to love, honour and obey in sickness and in health.

When should you give up hoping that person will treat you with love and respect.

Well let me now talk to you about my relationship with hope.

Hope, how dangerous is it. Perhaps the most dangerous of emotions if you are dealing with someone with NPD. Well for me, it was the hope that caused me the most anguish.

My friend had given me a beautiful white hydrangea flower for my wedding. I used to look at it, as a symbol of my marriage. When I watered it, I thought it was like the love I gave my husband. Taking on the advice from many books - "to work" at my marriage. To feed it, like I fed the flower. That in time, the sun and the water would bring it back to life. This plant would sometimes bloom with beautiful flowers and I would trick myself into seeing a mirror of that in my marriage. A good moment of an hour in a period of drought in two weeks, I would work on making that last for two hours the next time.

Then we moved house and I got a spade and dug up the flower and moved it to my new house and garden. And the trauma of the move, meant the flower nearly died. But I would just still see the odd green leaf a glimmer of life in the dying flower. Hydrangeas look like they are completely dead in the winter, but then come to life in the summer bearing the most beautiful flowers.

So I would look at this flower in the front garden, every day. Wondering if in some spiritual way, it was a reflection of the health of my marriage – a message from God about how relationships go through cycles, good and bad, sometimes bearing fruit and life, sometimes going through a drought.

Looking at the hydrangea every day or so waiting for shoots of life, as if it were connected. And this was the waste – this was the hope, this was the illusion and delusion.

This plant now has beautiful flowers on it, but that just means nothing.

I followed the advice to talk about feelings, to avoid fault and blame, and to always seek negotiation understanding and compromise. And I did this until my body, heart and soul ached with fatigue.

I thought my marriage was a living breathing thing that could grow, develop, be fed and could change. Every couple has there ups and downs, it's a journey of give and take. All those sayings you hear, you take them on board. You live them. That people have dark times and they come out of it.

But this was all drivel, complete and utter drivel that led me to waste a good 7 years of my life. A time when I was a young woman - beautiful, caring and fun. All the love, laughter, hope and care, went down into a deep dark hole of nothingness. The hole filled with no hope, the hole that just went down and down and down into an abyss. An abyss of nothingness, like the soul of my husband, devoid of love and care. Because he had not been given love and care.

I cannot tell someone to not hope, but for me it was a terrible waste. It delivered nothing, but then that is my story which I will now share with you.

CHAPTER 3 1997

I am going to go into quite a lot of detail about how I met my husband and how we had two relationships. A very brief one in 1997 and then again in 2006. I think this is important in setting the context of the story. In understanding how these relationships start and then change.

It was 1997, I thought I had met my prince charming, well he was a prince charming - literally come to life. Like all small girls who read about the fairy tales of Cinderalla, Snow White and Rapunzel. There comes a day that you look forward to, through your childhood and teenage years when you hope to meet your true love, your prince. He and you will just know in that moment that you are both meant to be, it will be cosmic, electric, a meeting of souls. Something will just feel right, the moment you have been waiting for all your life - when you meet "the one" your soul mate, a mirror image.

All those dreams you have, the desire to fall in love, that incredible feeling. That longing for happiness, a simple dream.

That man you meet who makes you feel special, straight away. That was my future husband who I will call Simon. And that happened.

In a very crowded bar at my university. Simon got stuck in the crowd right next to me. We started talking. He was gentle, and had the most incredible endearing way about him. Playful, romantic, sweet. He would bring his head down and his eyes up, and he seemed so happy and carefree. We laughed and got drunk with my group of friends.

Thinking back to this very first meeting, he was different. In some way he seemed more tuned into what I was saying, more mature than most men. More focused. And these mannerisms were unusual and very appealing and attractive. Vulnerability I guess, like a little boy.

That night, he said - it feels like I have known you and your friends for a very long time. He noted how strange that was, but he mentioned it like a "coming home".

He wrote, he called, he created a mixed tape of music on a cassette, he said he couldn't stop thinking about me. I liked him a lot, but he made me feel much more, much more quickly than I usually would. I was taking it easy, I had a life and friends, but he was intense – he was drawing me in. He made me feel like he was addicted to me, that I was a drug he couldn't live without. I really liked that, and I felt something deep for him very quickly

I was feisty, independent, fun, opinionated, sociable and all of a sudden I was weak in surrender to this love bombing. I was special, he made me feel so special. He needed to see me, he needed to talk to me. The first man to ever send me flowers.

He lived about an hour and a half away from where I was studying at university and he invited me to stay over after about 2/3 weeks of dating. He had just left home at 23 and bought a house.

He picked me up from the train station and we went to his parents house to pick up a pizza and a bottle of wine.

His parents owned a huge detached cottage in a very affluent area. It had land, a large drive and they were clearly very well off.

We walked through one of the entrances to the house, through the door into the kitchen, Simon winked at me as he grabbed one of his Mums expensive bottles of wine. Then he heard her call out to him, she was in the lounge. She didn't know I was there. I was in the kitchen, I could see him but not her.

And this moment I will remember forever and it was the moment I should have turned away and never looked back.....

It is one of those moments that is quite hard to write about and think about. As it has had a huge and fundamental impact on my life because it was a huge red flag and I didn't heed the warning.

It is just something that happened, but now I can see that if I knew what I know now, had I paid more attention to that incident, I could have saved those 20 years of my life. 20 years wasted on hope.

"Simon come here" no hello, no how are you.

"Don't wake your grandmother, do not go in your room. I have put your alarm clock where she is sleeping, don't get it out. When are you going to do this... This is happening....Don't you dare go up to your room and wake your grandmother. While we are on holiday I have left you a list of things to do, do not forget any of them"

What I can remember is seeing Simon frightened with his head bowed down. He stood there in silence, belittled and scared by a tirade of orders barked at him. Threats to not do this, and expectations of what was required from him.

His Mum did not know I was there, through all of this. I am glad of that now, because I got to see the real dynamic between mother and son. I got to see a real narcissist in her home environment abusing those she should have loved.

I then felt very uncomfortable she didn't know I was there, so I walked into the lounge. I was going to confront her, how dare she talk to Simon like that. I was really angry, she was so cruel. But I'd only been seeing him for a few weeks and it was too bold a move for me, at just 20 years old, I didn't have the courage.

I walked into the lounge to face her, she quickly appeared a little embarrassed and back tracked. "Oh hello, I didn't know there was anyone there, Simon didn't say (well Simon didn't have a chance to speak between the tirade of orders and expectations). Very nice to meet you." She said.

And then came lots of nice questions and interest about who I was, and a completely different person to the one I had witnessed as I stood in the dark kitchen.

She had no colour, and no flair in her clothes. A confident stare, and a detached way about her. This detachment is something I have become very sensitive to, I can see it now in other people. Their body and face are there, but their eyes and soul are somewhere else. Talking and talking, but the talking is not connected to themselves. That is a strange way to put it, but the best way I can describe it. You can see a kind of detached glaze in their faces and eyes.

The reason this incident was so significant was that 15 years later when Simon and I went to see a psychotherapist for marriage counselling she explained that you treat your partner how you were treated as child. And in that small window of time back in 1997 I would have been able to predict how I'd be treated as a wife.

After meeting his Mum, Simon and I then went to his new house which was about a10 minute drive away.

I discovered that his Mum had paid the deposit on the house and had chosen the furniture, and had chosen the house. She went with him to the house viewings. She also got him his job, had seen the advertisement and had encouraged him to go for it.

Back then when a story was told, I just listened, no more than that. It was just him telling me about his life and what his Mum had done. But now I can see how controlling that behaviour was.

I remember all was very well – Simon still happy, I was happy.

In the morning, everything had changed. Overnight he had left, like his spirit had lifted from his body, he wasn't there anymore. And I hope you read on, for me to tell you what happened later on in my life and how this exact same pattern was repeated over a longer period of time. But it has taken me a very long time to recognise the pattern and understand it.

I had fallen, from being up on high, adored, desired and then scrambling to get that feeling back. I could see he was no longer interested and didn't want me there. The intense flattery and charm had turned in an instant.

From a sunny day to a cloudy one, from warm to cold. He said my eye brows were too thin, and had been over plucked. I remember wearing cheap plastic boots with laces and the material was peeling, and he said that I shouldn't be wearing them and should throw them away.

It was like being on a pedestal and having it knocked away from under me, and then all of a sudden I'm sitting on the floor in a daze wondering what is happening. How something so sudden, so confusing could happen, did it happen?

Then you want to believe it is temporary, how can someone feel so much – be so genuinely interested and then feel nothing. But not just feel nothing, show no real interest or care.

They say the opposite of love is not hate, it is indifference. Like you are invisible, you are not even worthy of being acknowledged. This was the same situation I would suffer many many years later.

I was feeling desperate inside, but didn't want to give too much emphasis on those thoughts as it would then make it real. It was temporary surely?!

I carried on being my same self, happy, fun, chatty. But then he had changed, so I thought it must be me, I have changed. He doesn't like me anymore I did something.

What did I do? I look the same, I sound the same. But like milk that suddenly goes off, I had gone off. I felt rotten, I had turned rotten.

That shift from being idolized to being devalued. Is beyond comprehension when you feel like you might be falling in love. You then fall into despair.

Disorientating is the best way to describe it. From feeling like you heart is dancing full of love you feel a knot inside you. For me it was like I had been stabbed and the knife was still there. That feeling lasted for years, it turned into something else, but it stayed with me.

I thought I would be able to detect a con man. I had a good upbringing a wonderful Father, a strong sense of what was right and wrong and what was true. I thought I would never be so stupid to fall for it. I can spot someone when they are not being genuine.

We've all had our hearts broken, but what makes one heart ache worse than the other. The longer the relationship? I had only been seeing him for about 6 weeks when this happened but it went on to affect me for nearly 10 years.

That seems utterly ludicrous, writing that down now for you all to read, it is crazy, but it was the feeling he gave me at the start. That feeling no one else had really managed to. That I was special, why was I so receptive to that.

A deep sense of low self esteem? My mum had always used to say to me as I was growing up, "who's looking at you" when talking about myself in relation to others, i.e. the clothes I wore, and what I did. She suggested no one really cared or was looking, I guess she was right ultimately.

They don't care, they might compare themselves to me, to make themselves feel better. We can be over sensitive to how we are viewed by other people and in many ways she was right. But maybe I felt insignificant deep down. My Mum had not made me feel special and this man had?

He was aware of my deepest desires and needs, and he met them. Reflected upon who I was, and filled that empty space.

What was it, that made me so desperately unhappy when it was over. It was bliss when it was good, then utter despair when it was over.

I think when I am writing this, whether people will be able to identify with this or not. Is this a similar experience?

It was true and gut wrenching heart break you never seem to be able to shake off.

It was so intense that it did stay with me in all future relationships, it faded but it wasn't until I met someone else who evoked similar emotions of intense attraction, that I felt I was able to let him go.

Maybe I was just a sad case. I have heard of people not being able to get over an ex, but not me? Surely not me. I am a strong and independent career woman. But alas, it was me, he head broken my heart and I thought about him on and off for many years.

The relationship was over in just six weeks. He'd ended up chatting up my best friend on my 21st birthday and then went out with her about a year later. I was devastated and never really got over it.

CHAPTER 4 2006

When social media came along I had the perfect opportunity and excuse to reconnect with my lost love, to calm that ghostly pining I'd had for him for so long. Back in 2006 Friends Reunited was an active and growing platform for reconnection with friends of the past, so that is how I got in touch with him. I was hoping to find out he was married – really for the purpose of closure, to put that ghost of the past to rest. But he wasn't, he was single.

And he seemed quite delighted that I had got in touch, and then the flirting and back and forth emails began, as they do.

I was living in a flat in Southampton and I remember clearly the first time we spoke on the phone for the first time in 10 years.

I remember being nervous, I wanted him, but I didn't want him. I couldn't go back there, that much hurt, how could I possibly go back? I knew he could hear I was hesitant and reluctant to meet up, but that seemed to make him want me more.

For a man like Simon who I knew liked the challenge, I was a desirable prize. I was single, 29, had a fantastic career. He was smitten again, and I was flattered but I couldn't risk going there again.

But after 12 months of resisting I eventually gave in. He was that perfect person again, but this time the idealisation phase lasted a lot longer.

That feeling I had pined for all those years, it was back. I was completely lost in him. I was beautiful, successful, confident. I had a great job in the media. I knew I was a catch, I had lost weight. I was stunning and young and happy, intelligent and fun.

He started to mirror me. My beliefs, my desires, my thoughts, they were all matched by him.

So we started a normal courtship all over again, me 29 and he was 31. Neither of us had children, we were young, free and in love.

The relationship was going incredibly well. But I of course, was very scared about getting too involved and being hear-broken all over again.

For a long time, (about 12 months) I just enjoyed it, but as more and more time passed, and this is a very important point – it was our probation period.

After being incredibly cautious, he was taking his time to be everything I wanted again; kind, honest, patient. So I was starting to think he had changed, that this man would not break my heart (again).

So I felt I had tested him and he had passed. I was starting to want him like he wanted me, but more importantly I started wanting a future with him. I was getting ready to need him, to make a commitment.

People are weak, they make mistakes, people are not perfect but most of the time they have an ability to see when they have hurt people, when they are wrong. They may not know why they made those decisions that hurt others, but they are sorry for it.

Simon had left a string of broken hearts behind him when I met him. He didn't know why he was really "into" a girl then suddenly lost interest.

He was infatuated with numerous woman but it would all end the same way, with him losing interest eventually. I thought he was a commitment phobe. I read every book under the sun." the Rules of dating" books on commitment phobia, emotional unavailability but I don't think any of them really hit the nail on the head. They were helpful in their own way. And why did I need to read, did it help me make up my mind on what was going on, whether I could trust a man who had never had a proper relationship before me, a man who had very badly broken my heart and everyone else's before.

Some people don't listen to the whispers when a relationship starts, they ignore the red flags – that silent tapping on the shoulder and whispering in your ear – be ware. But I wasn't stupid and I thought his past would be a reflection of the future.

But I have to say I eventually gave in, after 18 months of this courtship with only a few concerns from my end, surely and slowly I caved in, I gave in.

Then there was the transition from perfection to horror, which I am about to continue to tell you about. That cognitive dissonance that horrendous confusion, that blindness and fog and complete and utter disorientation. That is something that not many have commented on. Not many who have been through this situation can really comment on it, they read about it. But to experience it, is quite hard to put in words. Like falling very fast and deeply into a black hole but not realising you are.

5 THE TRANSFORMATION

This is the moment that the charming man becomes the monster – although monster isn't really the right word. How can a monster kill with silence? This type of abuse is total withdrawal and disapproval, and the only time they speak is to disagree with you or subtly put you down, or deny your deserved pride and achievements.

This monster was a destroyer of the soul and self. To quietly and slowly tell you, that every opinion you have is wrong, everything you are proud of is nothing. Constantly challenging everything about you, but in such a subtle way.

Picking up on the state of the house seems to be a common theme. Any crumb on the carpet, cutlery not put away properly. There is always something to criticise and complain about. But at the time I just thought this was normal life as a couple, and I waited for the good times, but they became few and far between.

What happened to me was very slow, and difficult for me to see let alone anyone else. An erosion of my self confidence and belief in what was right and wrong. I didn't trust my gut, the way I do now.

Everyone has arguments, yes, but what makes it abuse. When does it just turn from not getting on, to something more corrosive and damaging? Sometimes something you can't come back from, because your belief in yourself has been eroded, when you can no longer make those judgements anymore.

Ok so how did this happen. How did my prince charming turn into the prince of misery.

It all started to happen when I moved in with him. I was already 8 months pregnant. I could not have been happier to be having a baby. As I described in the last chapter we had been courting for nearly two years he had pursued me doggedly, getting me to commit, to move in. Then here I was in his flat, he'd finally captured me and got what he wanted.

I was pregnant and off work, looking forward to a new baby together. The dream was realised.

Everything I had ever wanted, the perfect man, a beautiful child on the way. And oh my God it was just awful- straight away, I could see something drastically had changed, all of a sudden.

He wasn't there, is the only way I can describe it. Like a quiet withdrawal. An absence, a complete absence in fact of his presence. I just felt I have to do something here, this does not make any sense, where has my perfect man gone, exactly the same panic I had experienced back in 1997 when he lost interest after our short 6 week relationship.

I thought maybe he's sulking because I've done something wrong, or it will just take time to adjust to a new baby. He is in shock, he's never lived with anyone before. All those things were going through my head.

We went shopping in preparation for the baby, I was so excited. That is part of that thrill of having a baby, picking out nappies, cots, clothes, push chairs. It is such an exciting time, one you look forward to. But again he was like a walking corpse. It was worse actually than being on your own. Being with someone who has "opted out", just there out of duty and obligation but nothing else.

It is worse than being on your own because it actually makes you feel lost and alone, and depressed, desperately trying to reach out for that person to enjoy the experience with you. So you are not focusing on being happy and the future, but pulling that other person into the situation to enjoy it with you.

Is that abuse? No people don't think it is. It is not being hit, or screamed at or threatened. How many people live with that? How common is that? I think it is very common, but people don't see it. And that is why I am writing about it.

So when I talked to my family about my concerns they would say;

"He's just a bit sulky" or "It's going to take a lot to get used to a new situation"

But what my friends and family didn't realise, is that when I told them how sad I was and how desperate things were. They thought it was just now and again, that sometimes things would be good between us. But they weren't really, it was like this all the time.

They had assumed I was only talking about the bad days, and that there were good days. But I was unable to see that it was bad all the time, I honestly think it was shock, a trauma that I wasn't even present in the situation.

Cognitive dissonance is the best way to describe it, there weren't any good days. It was awful all the time and I had no idea why.

My family and friends had met Simon and I don't think they believed me, as he was a very different person around them. So when they didn't believe me, I didn't believe me. That is when you start to lose trust in your own gut instinct. When the people you love, validate what you are saying and thinking.

He was very charming to them and emotionally abusive to me. But I had never even heard of emotional abuse before.

They didn't see any bruises on my body, I know they love me, but I am sure they put it down to general nagging and an adjustment period after having a baby. I know my parents marriage was similar, and another reason why I normalised this behaviour and stayed in it.

It was not unfamiliar to me.

When my family came to visit, Simon was different. He was friendly, charming, warm. But when they left, he was back to that sullen, quiet, angry man.

Do you know what I really thought if I am honest with myself. I thought I deserved this, there is something wrong with me.

I made attempts to leave him, but I didn't actually have the courage within myself to go through with it. I would talk to my family and friends, but was hesitant to leave because of a feeling of shame.

I thought I would be disappointing myself, and I felt society's expectation is to have a family where both parents are present. Or basically if you can't manage that you are a failure.

I didn't want the shame of ending a relationship with a man I'd had a baby with, and I thought I could fix it. I fix everything.

When I look back and think about the life, what happened every day and the many incidents that took place, it was a very gradual and insidious destruction of self – my self.

I know back then that I'd get angry, I'd argue with his logic, to find a stand point that might get through to him. First I tried reason, then emotion. All the relationship handbooks and advice, the advice from Relate (where we went for counselling). A lot of the advice is to say how you are feeling. I read so much to try and find a solution.

This is the kind of thing I would read over and over again on websites. This is from Relate:

When you're annoyed with your partner, it can be tempting to act as if everything is their fault. We don't like to acknowledge that every disagreement has two sides to it – and it can be difficult to accept that there may be whole lot of stuff we could be doing to make things easier.

But you're much likely to be able to resolve problems if you take responsibility for your part in them.

If you find yourself phrasing concerns in terms of what your partner could be doing differently, saying things like 'you always' or 'you never', stop – and try using 'I' words instead: 'I feel', 'I would like' and so on. This will help you focus on your own feelings – and communicate to your partner that you're willing to see both sides of the discussion.

I followed this advice. We paid to see a Relate counsellor early on in the relationship when things became so difficult.

I said "I feel" I never accused, I was gentle. I really listened to this advice and followed it, but it didn't work. It just didn't work – and why?! This made me feel desperate.

It was then I would try everything and anything to get through to Simon. I would say sorry even when I knew it didn't feel right. I would just try everything I could to get back a bit of closeness and intimacy which I began to crave.

Sometimes I would get the closeness back but it would only last a day, then in time, it would only last a few hours. That closeness was my reward, and then as soon as I hadn't locked the garage door, or not cleaned the microwave after using it, or some other totally ridiculously minor thing, the closeness was taken away.

That detachment, the withdrawal, he used this to punish and control me and it would last longer and longer and it got progressively worse.

I tried and tried and tried. I cried and cried and cried. The frustration was overwhelming, I felt like progress had been made, but it was always temporary.

At the time, all I felt was totally and utterly and overwhelmingly haunted, by the past. All I thought about over and over again, was the man I fell in love with.

How he would buy my favourite blueberry muffins before I arrived for a weekend to see him. The time we tried to barbeque shell fish on his balcony. It was the most magical time, he was the most perfect gentleman.

Romantic, attentive, tolerant, forgiving, understanding, interested in everything I had to say. Vulnerable, really vulnerable, open sensitive. Great fun, playful. Everything I could ever have wanted and more. This was all without being soppy, he remained still strongly centered. He appeared to have strength as well as vulnerability. I never thought he seemed too good to be true, I simply thought he was the "one".

The feeling he gave me, no one else had given me. I remembered that short period we went out in 1997. It was happening all over again, 9 years later. He made me feel loved and special and truly adored. He made me feel beautiful.

That is what haunted me. That is what I thought about almost every few minutes, where has that person gone? It must be temporary I kept telling myself, I can bring this back around. This is my fault I thought, I can sort this.

I had no reason at the time to record in any great detail those incidents, I can remember them, visualise them. I thought well this is a rational and reasonable person, this must just be a temporary thing. I never thought that the person I fell in love with (before the baby came along) was not real. But as I explain later in the book, that man was not the real Simon.

An example would be. I bought some reduced chicken from the local shop, it was still in date, but it really smelt when I opened and it was green. I said I am going to call the shop and tell them, as they don't want to sell this to someone else. He said angrily "why would you do that, why would you waste your time." Then stormed out of the room.

Or when his colleague caught fish as a hobby and gave some to us which we kept in the freezer. I said I wasn't sure about giving it to our son who was under two at the time as I didn't know how long it had been out of the water. He stood up and started shouting at me, saying this was a ridiculous thing to say and the fish was fine and then he stormed out and slammed the door.

Another example, it was a beautiful sunny day and our son was just 6 months old and we went for a walk in a stunning local park. We had the day off and it was gorgeous weather. The flowers were all out, everyone was smiling. I was looking forward to going out as a family. I had just bought a second hand pushchair from ebay. The bars on it were too low and I was struggling to push it. I got it out of the car and said this is rubbish it's going back on ebay. And he went into one of his rages.

To describe one of these rages, it is like a seething anger, his face frozen, rigid. His body rigid. He said "so what about me, what if I want to keep it" and I said of course that is fine in a calm way. And then for the entire day he did not speak to me.

I said to him, that it was crazy. And he continued to say over and over again, that I was being unreasonable, by making decisions without him.

I suppose I believed his version and not mine, and this carried on for so many years.

What would usually happen in these situations that became huge rows, was that he would go into a rage over something very small and insignificant and then I would get angry back. I thought getting angry back was the right thing to do – to fight my corner and show that I was not a door mat. In time I learnt something very important, and that was to look at the irrationality of the situation before reacting. As in this case, I didn't like a pushchair and wanted to put it back on ebay.

That is a perfectly acceptable and normal opinion. I had done nothing wrong, so getting angry back was pointless. You only get angry back to defend yourself, I had nothing to defend. I had done nothing wrong, but at the time I could not see that.

I would make the mistake of getting angry and shout and call him names, and then he would turn it around on to me, and make me feel guilty for my reaction.

I learnt in time to stand back and watch and not get angry back. By getting angry back you are validating what has just happened, you are giving power to nonsense. It is as if you can't see the irrationality of the other. And it is insane.

You don't argue back, you stand back, that is the best way of dealing with it. But you need to work on, knowing what is crazy behaviour and what is not. That is what can take time. Especially if you have seen crazy behaviour as a child.

But back then in the park, I didn't know all of this, I did not have this knowledge. He won me over and convinced me and I trusted his view on this – he brought me around, he persuaded me, but there was this niggling doubt inside of me where I thought this is crazy. But I must have had such a weak sense of self, of what was ok and what was not ok, that I listened to him.

That I thought fair enough my punishment is being ignored all day and I deserve it somehow. Having to walk around this beautiful park with my gorgeous baby with a man who is so angry he can't talk to me.

I also felt that was his right, to behave as he wished. I still thought he was that man I fell in love with. I thought I must be doing something wrong here. This guy is great deep down. I wouldn't have fallen in love and had a child with him otherwise. Cognitive dissonance and my upbringing are the two reasons I stayed in this situation for as long as I did. Those two things I will explore in more detail later.

Basically now looking back, I can see it was always the same. I would express an opinion, and he would blow up. We went to see a house that needed a lot of work, and met the previous owner there who recommended a builder. He was very suggestive and flirty with me and made me feel uncomfortable. As we left I said I wouldn't be happy using the builder he recommended and that he was a bit sleazy.

Simon exploded into a rage and started bashing the steering wheel with great force. Saying "but he arranged to meet us, he did us a favour, he didn't have to do that" an explosive rage, where he hit things, he didn't hit me but he hit things. He scared me.

Why didn't I see the behaviour at the time as deranged? Well I know that I did, I did think it was deranged and I remember it really well. This was 7 years ago and I remember it like it was yesterday. I was in shock, that rage he went into – so quick, and it came out of nowhere. It was the kind of rage you get, if you cheated on your partner.

Something where you really have done something wrong and you know you are going to get it. These incidents would happen over and over again.

Something very insignificant and he would blow. I was never hit, not once. All these minor incidents. Where I would do something that should have only slightly annoyed him but his reaction was if I had just had an affair or spent all our money and got us into terrible debt.

Over time it got worse. He would throw things, or kick things sometimes, very frequently slammed doors. Smashed the glass out of the oven door. Left a huge dent in the dishwasher. But most of the time it was just an intense rage followed by days and weeks of silence. The silent treatment, the most cruel punishment of all that makes you feel invisible and totally worthless. (please read Patricia Evans book on verbal abuse which helped me to see this)

The silent treatment went from lasting a day, to a few days and then to a few weeks. I would always be holding on and longing for the warm and caring Simon to come back. I would ask what I needed to do, to resolve the situation.

He would give me an answer and then I would try it. But then he said he couldn't just move on that quickly. So even when I listened and tried to do as he said, i.e. do as I was told and never get angry. I cleaned up all those things that used to irritate him so much, like the oven, microwave, making sure I locked the door. These were the things that used to get him so angry, and would result in that punishment.

Once when my eldest son was potty training, we left him without a nappy on in the garden. And he ended up pooing in the shed. I shouted to Simon come and see, I was laughing. And Simon shouted at me, he was really angry. "Why did you let him do that. It's not funny, why doesn't he have a nappy on" imagine those words in a really angry tone of voice.

I could fill this book with incidents like that. They were daily. But I hung on in there, as I wanted that drug I suppose. That incredible high I had, when we were together in that first period.

I would argue back, I thought we were just arguing. But I wouldn't really hear and see what was going on, that the first statement he made was bonkers. I guess I didn't know it was bonkers so I counteracted it with a reply, a response that then turned into an argument.

I should have just realised you don't get angry with someone for having a different opinion.

I would always try to get him to see my point of view, using emotional or logical means. Neither ever worked. I was always in the "wrong" and feeling in the wrong for so long is going to have an impact on your sense of self and self esteem. He would never say, ok yes I guess you are right this time. Or sorry.

I can remember just two occasions in our relationship where he said sorry. Quite a few people have said that to me about the partner they are with. What a huge danger sign that is because it means that person never thinks they have made a mistake and let's face it everyone makes mistakes.

The number of times I would go over an argument, tossing it and turning it in my mind, so confused, trying to remember what was said.

I used to think well maybe I should not have said that, and I would always come down hard on myself and end up saying sorry. But it was usually because I was presented with rage over a minor incident that I would respond with rage. So I then ended up apologising for my rage. This was because I was desperate to get some kind of intimacy and closeness back.

Knowing what I know now, I would change my reaction, now I can see straight away that this is the behaviour of a narcissist. But at the time, when Simon would get angry I would get angry and abusive back. The problem then would be, that I could never be quite sure who should say sorry, so invariably I always did.

I said sorry, and in that I diminished myself. I said sorry just to get some relief from the silent treatment. The sulking that would go on for days and days and weeks and weeks and in the end years. There was no respite from the sulking in the end. There might be a reprieve for a few hours, where he would talk to me in a normal relaxed and happy way. But those moments were rare and became rarer as time went on.

If he was going away for the weekend or for a night out I would see a change in his behaviour he could be excited and optimistic. But never before he went away for a weekend or night out with me.

For my birthday I planned a very expensive hotel stay which cost me a lot of money. I was really looking forward to it. We didn't argue but the whole time, he was flat. He was terrible company, there was no laughter or fun. It wasn't romantic. It was like going on a business trip with someone who "had" to be there. The whole time away I was trying to please him, trying to bring him back to life, get that energy back into him.

How confusing for me, because I thought that person I first met was the real person. It has been extremely disorientating for me to realise that the real person was in fact the second person I met who was always angry and displeased and withdrawn.

I diminished myself, I lost all sense of who I was. I doubted "real events", I questioned every word I said. I felt low, I had no self worth.

I struggle now looking back on those years and think about the effect it has had on my son who is now 7. That he saw all that anger and frustration. That I was so beautiful, kind and full of love and hope and adventure and talent. But those 7 years were totally wasted. I am not perfect, but I really didn't deserve that and neither did my son.

I see patterns of behaviour in my son, which mirror that relationship I had with Simon. That when a drink is spilt all over the floor, it is someone's "fault" that it didn't just happen. That whenever basically anything goes wrong, or is broken it is always someone's fault.

He's becoming withdrawn like his father, and aggressive and a bully to his little brother. It is horrific to admit because I gave up everything for my son. I could not have loved my child more. I wanted the very best for him. And now I see those terrible traits and I don't know how to undo them. My perfect sweet innocent boy who has been poisoned by this, who I should have protected, who is now closed off a lot of the time and has no idea of what a happy loving relationship between two people should look like.

He can't play with his brother and sister very much, he doesn't seem to know how. He survives in his own company just like his father did. He didn't see his Mum and Dad laughing, or holding hands, or kissing, or talking, or arguing and seeing those arguments being resolved.

He didn't see his Dad ever saying sorry. He didn't see the warmth and depth, the beautiful complexity of those human relationships where there are ups and downs and people say sorry and they get close and they rely on each other.

Even now after what I have been through I would struggle to be with someone else. I'd like to in a way to show my eldest son who is now 7, that this is possible. But I feel so damaged, I don't think yet I could let another person into my life.

Hope in making a relationship with a narcissist work, was wasted hope for me. But hope that you can repair from the experience and have a normal relationship again is a hope that is worth devoting yourself to.

So will I meet someone else one day? They say from 0 - 5 is such an important age, where we learn about love and attachment and trust. My son had the attachment of both me and his father. But he never had a positive experience of what a relationship should look like, and if I can, I would like to turn that around and give him that good example.

At the end of the day not everyone is a covert narcissist.

Later in the book, I will discuss how I was able to reignited that hope I'd meet someone else and fall I love again, by realising the following.

My ex-husband did not have positive attachment growing up and that is why I don't hate him. I can see it very clearly now. It is very hard to hate someone, to feel bitterness and anger when you meet their Mum (my mother in law) and you wonder how this woman was ever allowed to keep a child in her care.

That is what is so hard to grapple with now. But that is why this book is being written. I want other people to see this pattern and to identify it.

6 COVERT ABUSE

Silence and gas-lighting for me were my ex husbands favourite weapons of control.

It is my belief that this kind of domestic abuse is rife, and it's not just women or men being abused physically. They are being ignored, shunned, constantly feeling that nothing they do is right, walking on eggshells. Never finding resolution, apologies never given. This kind of abuse is not given a lot of attention in the media, but I do truly believe it is a huge problem within many marriages and partnerships.

I have read a lot about cognitive dissonance and I think it is why covert narcissist partners get away with this type of abuse for so long. Certainly this was the situation for me.

Cognitive dissonance is when you can't relate the past experience to the current one. It is disorientating. The person that made you feel so special, who brought magic and love to your life suddenly turns into a cruel uncaring withdrawn person who just criticises you all the time.

That you just hang on for those moments or flashes, when they show you a little bit of what they were like before, just enough to keep you hanging on in there.

The three common stages of a relationship with a narcissist are idealise, devalue and then discard. I guess I was hooked on the idealise phase. It appealed to my ego I guess, my fragile ego that needed that boost. It was pure vanity. He made me feel the most beautiful and incredible creature in the world.

That feeling was so addictive. There has to be a lot to say about me and a lot for me to reflect upon to understand why I was so drawn to that, and could not see that it wasn't realistic.

So I was hooked on the first stage of the relationship with the covert narcissist so when the devalue and discard came, I didn't see it. I had that disconnection and detachment, that dissonance.

So this is where I talk about this very insidious and rarely talked about form of domestic abuse. So much damage can be done with silence.

I would have lunch, a sandwich or something and three hours later I would look in the mirror and see I had some food on my chin or cheek or a big black bit of spinach in my teeth. I'd think, well I've spoken to Simon a lot since then and he didn't mention it.

I'd walk around naked and he wouldn't even turn his head.

Sometimes the abuse was not that he had insulted me, he had not criticised me. So I didn't feel I had any right to be upset or angry. He was just being himself, so I really did feel I was invisible and worthless. I started to think that it wasn't a distorted opinion he had of me, but I really wasn't attractive enough to be looked at. That I wasn't worthy enough to be told I had food on my face.

You start doubting your own reality when you are around this kind of behaviour day in day out. Another thing Simon would do, is tell you passionately something had happened that did not happen. That I would recount an incident that I was sure really happened and he would say I had remembered it wrong. They call this gas lighting.

That makes you doubt your own reality so that when further abuse happens, you don't really know that it is happening to you. I don't think he realised he was doing it, it never felt like he had sinister intentions. It almost felt like he was just wanting to have power and control over me. That it was a subtle thing, that perhaps he was not even aware of it himself.

He really was convinced something happened in a certain way, and I was convinced too. But somehow his version became more of a reality for me and I stopped trusting myself and my own memories and my own version of events.

I will give you an example that happened recently. I had to drop my eldest son off at scouts. It is in a hall inside a large church up a flight of stairs. I left my other two children in the car briefly and rushed in with him. Very often the scouts can meet at the park or the beach, or a farm for a special trip. So I get a bit paranoid that if I just let him walk into the hall there may be no one there. That I could have missed a message that it was elsewhere that night.

Well one day I dropped my son off, and took him up to the hall and I actually saw the other beaver scouts, I saw all of his friends running about. As I left quickly to get back to my other children waiting in the car, I really did doubt what I had seen. I became anxious that I had dropped him off in an empty hall. Even though I had seen with my own eyes his friends in the hall.

This was doubting my own reality. Something that would not have happened without those many years of insidious mind control in my relationship with a covert narcissist.

For me one of the most painful parts of this period in our relationship is the memories I have of my children growing up, as in I don't have any. I have brief visual moments but I cannot emotionally connect to the past. I think this is the effect of trauma. I cannot connect to memories of the past, because I was constantly in a state of fear, fight or flight. When I went to see a therapist to recover from this relationship this is the only time I cried, when I recounted how I had no memories of my children growing up.

It was going to see a psychotherapist that started the change, it was the change that was the beginning of a new life and freedom.

7 THERAPY

It was very difficult indeed to get Simon to therapy. As I had tried many different strategies to improve the situation, I really felt this was a last resort.

There were many excuses, it is too expensive, or who looks after the kids when we go, or I can't get time off work.

But finally I got him to agree. (I will explain later, how pointless it is to drag someone to counselling)

When we had seen counsellors in the past and he had rubbished their suggestions, conclusions and advice. Often using the excuse that they weren't qualified or experienced.

So I thought I would find the best therapist I could. The one I settled on had numerous qualifications including a PhD.

Her approach was integrative, which meant she could use any theory, such as looking into our past family relationships. Alternatively, she could use an existentialist approach and concentrate on finding coping strategies in the present. It basically meant she could adapt her counselling style to suit who we were and what we needed.

Not everyone wants to discuss their past, but they can be happy working in the present.

Well I had so much hope going to this first session.

The first thing she said was, the aim of these sessions is to get you to decide on whether you will stay together or separate.

She went on to explain this further by saying, while you may have come here, hoping these sessions will save your marriage. You may in time come to see that the best option is for the marriage to end.

I felt very sad when she said that, as I wanted our marriage to work out. But looking back now, she was right and thankfully that is what the counselling delivered.

One of the biggest issues with the therapy is that my husband didn't want to go. I have since discovered, from my own training to be a psychotherapist, is that if someone does not want to go - it is pointless.

This is because they don't have a goal, there is no desire to change, so what could they possible get out of it? You have to "want" something, for therapy to work.

I am still glad we went, because over just the four sessions we had together - the psychotherapist saw enough of our dynamic together to really help me and she did.

The therapist picked up on the fact that Simon was logical and I was emotional.

The therapist asked us about our parents, to which Simon said he thought his Mum had a personality disorder.

We only had four sessions together and we just argued - I thought it was pointless at the time, and after each one felt quite hopeless. But they were useful because they enabled her to see how we interacted.

After those four sessions she recommended that we had one to one sessions with her. Me one week and Simon the other.

And that is for me, when the real progress happened.

That is when she told me that Simon's only strategies appeared to be win/loose, fault and blame.

It took time for me to really get this.

He had to either win or lose an argument - so if he could only win or lose, those disagreements would never be resolved. They would always leave damage. So yes that made sense.

So what is a fact and what is fault.

Simon would get very angry all the time, and say everything was my fault.

For example, Simon would get very angry that our son wouldn't got to sleep, and this was my fault. Not a fact that he was full of energy for whatever reason and was not sleeping.

If the car broke down, it was my fault, Simon would say I had not driven it properly. In other words someone always had to be at fault. Things never just happened.

Distinguishing the difference between faults and facts was an important part of the process we went through in therapy, and enabled me to see that Simon saw things in a very toxic way.

Also during my one to one session the therapist said:

"You treat your partner as you were treated as a child"

That sentence I took with me as the most powerful and enlightening and it really helped me.

When we had been to couples counselling in the past (at Relate) they told us we needed to talk about feelings and to compromise and celebrate each others differences.

Thankfully, this woman who was a far more experienced counsellor and could spot emotional abuse very quickly, got to the heart of our relationship within a few sessions.

When I met her on my own, I talked about the two great years I had with Simon where I was very happy, followed by the six years where I was very unhappy.

I explained to her that I struggled to understand who he really was - the lovely man who I knew for 2 years. Or the horrible man I knew for six.

She indicated that the man I knew for 6 was the real Simon.

We talked at length about empathy. What it means to care for another.

What is interesting, is that I got very confused and angry.

It started to dawn on me, that I had been the victim of emotional abuse.

It was a real shock for me, as I had previously just felt Simon and I were not getting on.

But the books said to me I was a classic case of emotional and psychological abuse. That word abuse, triggered a lot of anger.

So during that period of counselling I was not calm, I was just angry.

When Simon had his session on his own with the psychotherapist I discovered that he did open up with her and show some vulnerability. But I bombarded him with questions, I was controlling and angry and wanted to know exactly what happened in the session.

I was not patient and perhaps progress albeit small could have occurred had I let the therapist do her job.

She had warned me that the whole process would be likely to take years, not months. I think she could see the issues from his past, meant this would be a long one.

This was a problem as Simon had been very strict about us only having 4-6 sessions.

He said he'd return if she felt he needed to, but there was the impasse - because she would not continue to see him unless he wanted to.

So he didn't go back and to be honest, deep down I didn't want the marriage anymore. I felt like a victim of abuse and just wanted to get away from him.

I was not patient, I was incredibly angry. And at that stage the therapy stopped and we agreed that he would leave and the marriage was over.

A year after my husband left I went back to therapy, because something awful had happened. I think I was becoming a narcissist.

8 CONTAGION

I realised that I had stopped feeling, as I'm training to become a psychotherapist and there is a lot of emphasis on being self aware, and I realised something was very different. My emotional reaction to things had changed, I was feeling very detached. For example I had stopped caring about the pet cat. As a child I'd had a cat from the age of 2 until 18, I adored "Tommy", he was my best friend, I used to let him sleep on my bed. I really loved the cat, I talked about him all the time.

So I was really looking forward to having a cat after Simon left. He was allergic to animals so it had never been an option before, so as soon as he left I got one. But I felt nothing but annoyance for the creature, I couldn't connect in compassion and care in anyway.

I saw it as I would see a piece of meat. I am not a vegetarian, and I would ponder in a logical way constantly how people would treat cats and dogs like a member of the family, while still eating bacon sandwiches and beef burgers, when cows and pigs are arguably just as intelligent as cats and dogs.

Yet we turn a switch on in our head, that makes us accept it as being ok. I don't have that switch anymore, everything is logical and reasoned. But there is something significant missing, I don't enjoy stroking the cat. I am struggling to enjoy anything.

I feel a bit like I am dead, I don't feel the things I once did. I don't feel enjoyment, but I also don't feel fear. I don't get scared or intimidated by people, I feel like I have my mind set on a higher plain. But I do want recognition and grandeur and I am distracted by fantasies of power and fame. Power to influence a lot of people in a positive way. But no hunger to find my own desire, to quench my own thirst for life, I see the whole of society not the individual anymore. And my children's happiness as my priority.

I don't want to feel, emotions have been shut off. It was my second session with a psychotherapist that I realised after all that time with a narcissist - a person without empathy, I was actually becoming one.

I also encountered the pain and distress as I began to become aware of what had happened and how I could not open my heart again to feel again. I could not give up the logical control of the mind to the power of the heart. To feel, would be to feel overwhelmed. I actually started to feel psychically ill when I contemplated it.

I realised I didn't want to feel again, so I didn't want to go to therapy. I couldn't possibly let that in.

I had been drinking every day, I tried to describe why. I said it was enjoyment, it made me feel something I suppose.

The psychotherapist it was an anti-depressant. Which I could not understand as I am not depressed, but I guess I don't feel joy. I do feel fine, I feel the same all the time. I feel in control and I much prefer that to feeling anything else, like out of control.

She explained there are three main emotions; anger, grief/sadness and happiness and joy and we often stop ourselves from feeling these emotions because we judge them. They have associations, i.e. good girls can't feel angry, can't get angry and that is what can stop us from feeling them.

I feel angry about my ex husband, for destroying a good 8 years of my life. For subjecting me to constant disapproval and criticism, never making me feel loved and accepted. Always making me feel that his anger was my fault. That I was never good enough.

I wish I had been stronger and left him sooner so I am angry with myself, but I am more angry with him for the emotional abuse I suffered for so many years.

I wanted to shout and kick and hit him, I really hated him. But there are two things that are stopping that anger from spilling over into action (ie shouting, screaming, hitting, insulting)

The first is that I recognise and understand the struggles he faced as a child with a mother who had NPD (narcissistic personality disorder) herself. But also the fact I had three small children with him, and I had to get on with him for their sake.

To this day he still talks to me with intense hatred and disrespect, and because the children are listening I ignore it and try and keep the peace. But there is a welling up of intense anger inside of me, I want to punch him and shout at him and make him suffer and I have to keep that intense anger buried deep inside. And maybe that is why I am numb.

They talk about grandiosity with narcissists. But now I have realised the effects of being with a narcissist and the affect that emotional abuse has had on me.

That I have detached from my feelings - so now I can feel what the narcissist felt like. The grandiosity thing is a confidence, I am very sure of myself. Everything I feel has a logical explanation, I feel so empowered.

I am drawn to power and influence, not so much money. But I am realising yes, I want people to look at me and think yes she is someone special, probably cos at the very heart of me, I feel so utterly worthless.

But I am not after money I know that. Has anyone heard of a self-aware narcissist. Or is that a contradiction in terms?

I am in a strange place, realising I have become like my husband in many ways. That I am cold inside and manipulative, that I don't feel the same way I used to. How I can sell a cat who has settled into my home, without feeling too much guilt. That I can disconnect from shame and guilt, but also joy.

I am always craving validation and recognition, but for something that can change lives. I want to changes lives now, it's not about money but I do want power.

But I don't want to go back to the person I am. I feel like I am reconstructing myself from scratch as if I have just been born.

The one thing I have developed, is huge self-awareness, I can logically see everything I feel. But I just can't feel what I feel.

When people talk of narcissists they look at the ESDM definition. But now I am aware of being a bit of a vampire, thinking all good in people is in fact bad. A deep cynicism of the world.

I think about what draws people to positions of power. CEO's, MPS, the leaders of government, business and media. Why do they want to be successful, it is power. They get off on the power. But to be successful you have to be ruthless, and sure of yourself. And these kind of personality traits are stronger in narcissists. So the people running the country are mostly narcissists in my opinion.

I can see this because I feel powerful now, like I can do anything. I know if I had to convince someone in a job interview to hire me, that I would get the job. I can mirror someone else's actions, their body language the things they say. I can see what they want me to say, what they care about and I can mirror that. It is about being slick, and charming and at times when needed, vulnerable. Because if you are vulnerable with someone, you are saying you trust them.

But it is a fake vulnerability, for you would never really be vulnerable again. That is the truth.

When you have been abused you can't be vulnerable again, it is simply too painful.

You learn to mirror, it is a means of survival to get what you want. This is how people get to the top, those in management, politics, leadership, the media. The people who have influence know how to play this game, possibly subconsciously. But it is a manipulation in order to get power, so why would someone be drawn to power - to be in charge of others. Because ultimately they feel powerless.

I have no fear and immense confidence. I could draw people in with my charisma, confidence and personality. I can take charge and make decisions with certainty. That is because I have no self-doubt. I am certain about what is right and wrong. I don't ask advice.

To ask advice is weakness, I can see everything clearly. I feel so powerful. I don't want to give all that up, to feel - to get those emotions that make me feel so vulnerable and shaky. I am talking genuine vulnerability here, not faked vulnerability that you turn on to charm. Genuine vulnerability is that uncertainty that comes over you in a wave, that destabilizes you. That overwhelms you.

I would describe it as having a wave crash over me, that my body gets swept away and I don't know where I will land or where my body will settle, I simply won't be in control anymore. I can't let those emotions in, when I started to try, I felt very ill. I would compare it to holding on to a metal railing next to the sea, and a wave crashes over me and I try so hard to keep my grip on this bar but the strength of the wave overwhelms me and I have to let go and then I am no longer in control.

The wave of emotion is in control and I am in a tsunami being bashed around the ground and into buildings. That is what it feels like to give up on this feeling of being in control and let the feelings in. An anger and despair that would drown me.

I am explaining all of this, because I believe I had developed the mind, heart and soul of a narcissist. If I could feel this, then maybe you can relate to it. If I could become a narcissist then anyone could. In other words it just happened, it is no one's fault. Somewhere along the line a narcissist gave birth to a narcissist and so on and so on.

During this period of my life where I had become emotionally numb, I had arranged to see the same psychotherapist once a week, and she was on holiday then for two. I felt like I needed therapy on a drip. I was unsteady, I drank more alcohol than usual. Like a hole in a damn and a crack was forming and growing, and all of a sudden it would all gush out.

The therapist described how I was in control of what feelings I wanted to feel, that I could in a sense, take a peak behind the curtain. Just for a second, and then maybe a few days later, peak again.

But I took a peak, and it was a feeling I didn't like so I can't see why I would go back to peaking again.

It caused me to feel very depressed. Well sadness is an emotion, I can see that is probably what should have happened and is completely normal. But it was horrible, I didn't want to feel that.

But I do listen to music now, all the time. That is connecting me to something, I never used to listen to music. Maybe that is the little peak into feelings I feel comfortable with for now.

I watched a lot of Sam Vankin on YouTube, a self confessed narcissist. When I watched him I never thought for a second, that I could also one day end up one. And now I am thinking, if I am honest, I'll get so much praise and recognition for this book. Why am I writing it? to make a difference in people's lives, or to get "off" on the power.

I do want others to become self aware, and to see those emotional vampires, those soul destroyers, who only think and do not feel. Then they can move on without hope that person will change. But I am seeing how the narcissist is born.

I am getting into a new relationship now, and there is no chance of me being committed, of being able to have a normal relationship. I don't know what a normal relationship is. I have no hope that this relationship will have a chance unless I change. I can see I need to change, that I am numb. But I don't want to.

I suffered a trauma that didn't happen in an hour or a day or a week. It happened over many many years. From the day my son was born in 2009 until 2016 when I broke free.

That is a long period to fight, to hope, to feel anguish. The therapist said it was a coping strategy, that is how I dealt with the situation I cut myself off from it. I cut myself off from the feelings and tried to make sense of it.

So I listened to her that first time my husband and I went to see her in 2014 for couples counselling, I listened when she said "you treat your partner how you were treated as a child"

That made sense, in my own life in how I treated my husband and how he treated me.

But I took that logic and it gave me all the hope I needed, the only answer I had. I clung to that, and followed it through. I looked in detail into personality disorders, my mother in law. What had she experienced as a child to make her so unbelievably cold and cruel, and how that had then impacted on my husband and his upbringing.

He was made to sit in the garage after school and wait for her, as she didn't trust him to have a key and let himself in. He was left to do a paper round at 5am in the dark cycling for miles without a helmet on down narrow country lanes. His family were incredibly wealthy, successful, middle class. But the parental neglect of a narcissist parent can be found in any home - rich or poor.

So my ex husband Simon had suffered, he didn't have the emotional love and care that I'd had.

I always searched for logical answers, trying to understand my husband's abusive and neglectful childhood, I didn't feel the despair. I had cried and shouted and sobbed too much and for too many years. That in the end I had to turn it off, for my own sanity. I had to turn those feelings off. A coping strategy.

He had turned his feelings off as a child, I can see now he had no choice. He couldn't even remember a lot of what happened to him as a child, even once describing it as a happy childhood. But over time I got to hear the truth. Snippets of stories, where he was forced to do things he didn't want to do, how he was humiliated or neglected time and time again.

His sister is also divorced, she became a withdrawn and absent wife until her husband could not tolerate it any longer. That is no coincidence that she was raised by the same mother, as my husband.

That is what my husband was essentially, withdrawn and absent. But also never happy and he made it very clear to me, that it was my "fault". That there was always something I was doing wrong, that meant he was never happy. Be that not putting the washing out when there was just enough sun in the day to dry it. Or not cleaning the oven or microwave after I used it, or buying bread when we didn't need it.

Not a small row, like healthy couples might have - where both move on within an hour or two, or a day if it's a really bad one.

He would not speak to me for a whole day. How many days did I waste being punished? Punished for the smallest most ridiculous thing. Punished for my very existence, punished for something that wasn't anybody's fault.

So what does it say about my self worth that I put up with that, and thought it was somehow justified.

That he would never want to have sex with me, and I would ask why? I always had the same answer because he couldn't just "snap" out of how he was feeling. That it wasn't natural for him to just quickly get over a row. But he never got over that row, he was sulking all the time.

44

Weeks and weeks passed, and then months without sex. I was so unhappy but accepted that was how he felt, and I had to respect that. I just kept hoping foolishly that he would one day forgive me, and love me again. Even though now, I can see I had not done anything wrong.

When I went into labour with my third child, something changed I'd had enough. I said to him that I didn't want to use these hangers that you put on the radiator, to dry your clothes.

I very calmly said that I'd tried them before and the clothes didn't dry. And he shouted at me, for having this view. Then he didn't speak to me all day.

That same day I went into labour with my third child, as I was getting contractions he was sitting in the bath with my eldest son. I said, "I'm going into labour" - and he didn't even look at me.

We got in the car and he didn't talk to me. I was experiencing those normal and intense labour pains, and he was sulking. I had no support, no love and no care. I felt all alone, I'd rather have been alone in fact. Instead I was thinking how could he be this cruel?

Another example that happened towards the end of our marriage. I had to call a paramedic as I had chest pains, as the GP surgery would not see me, I had to call 999. I texted him to say the ambulance had arrived and I was being checked over. And he texted back, as he was out, and said " do you mind if I take (our son) to legoland this Friday"

I told this story to the therapist, and when she was him the next week on his own, they discussed empathy. Did he have empathy? No I don't believe he really did, not for me anyway. Not for anyone, even for himself.

It always felt that I had done something extremely seriously wrong and I was being punished all the time. This seething hatred – silent treatment, silent hatred always bubbling under the surface that would sometimes explode into a rage.

My therapist said I had to get angry. But I can't. I just feel pity and sympathy for my husband. Because he cannot feel guilt or shame, or regret. He doesn't seem to have access to those kinds of feelings. He is not happy, he is very lost. So what is the point of being angry. And there it is again, what is the point of being angry. My logic takes the place of my emotion.

I am stopping the anger and controlling it. If the anger does take hold then I think it will overwhelm me. And that really is why narcissists can't let the feelings in, not unless they have constant therapy, therapy on a drip.

I feel the same now - not unless I have constant therapy, I am not sure how else I can do it. How can you let those feelings overwhelm you, when you haven't even felt them for a moment. For so long you cut them off.

I look back now to 2009 where my first child was born. I was sitting in the sunshine, with my new baby in my arms at a café. A woman commented on how beautiful my new baby was, and said "you must be so happy" and I smiled - a fake delicate smile, that hid the truth. Yes it should have been the happiest day of my life, it felt like it should have been. But I felt dispair, pure and utter despair.

If I was being beaten up, everyone would have seen the bruises, they would have saved me. But the abuse and violence was on the self. There were no bruises, I was becoming withdrawn just like the victims of psychical domestic abuse. But this was emotional and psychological abuse, and while I fought back I still felt. I had feelings. When I stopped fighting back and when I stopped hoping, that is when I stopped feeling.

But because he had been through it I forgave him, but at the same time I became numb.

You see lots of women on YouTube and other platforms talking about the narcissist in their life, their ex. I could not do this, for it humiliates the ex. They may eventually hear or see the videos, their friends or colleagues might find it. Therefore their dialogue is one of " they do this because they are bad people, they have no goodness inside them."

This would be their approach and agenda. I could not stand loud and proud talking about my ex who is a narcissist because that would be to humiliate the already deeply damaged and hurt individual. There is of course somewhere where they do feel pain, humiliation and shame. Do they need further reprehension and condemnation when often they have had this all through their childhood?

When do we stop being kind? no matter what these people have done to us. There could be nothing worse than....being them.

That does not mean we have to stay with them, but to forgive them will let us go. It will allow us to heal.

I have come out of that narcissistic black hole but when I was in it, it was very dark and very empty.

One example of that time, is when I stroked the cat, I didn't want to, I just did it for a very brief time because I felt sorry for it.

It feels like its existence is totally pointless. Perhaps if I was a true narcissist how I treat the cat is how I would treat my children. Maybe that is how my ex was treated by his mother. Given food, kept clean, but little warmth and love provided. Where all the practical needs are met but not the emotional.

My ex didn't seek out therapy, therapy only works if you have a goal - some kind of desire, "something" to work on. But if he has never felt any different, if he has always been numb, if he has always felt that nothingness inside of him what can he compare it with? Why would he seek change?

It is not realistic, you can't desire to feel, if you have never really felt. Or at least not since you were a very young child, during a period that you cannot remember.

I am going through that, I can see the change in me. Wanting alcohol to feel happy, not connecting to my children, not enjoying them. Not enjoying anything but things that feed my ego.

9 SOCIETY

Is it possible that most of our leaders are narcissists?

Let us consider, why a narcissist may make a good leader. First of all, they are certain in their decisions, and that inspires confidence. They don't need or seek external validation, they have internal validation.

I know that because that is how I feel now. I feel fearless, as if fear is a weakness - one of the many emotions I have purged since the long abusive episode. I feel invincible, all powerful.

The person working in a small shop, with a friendly smile on their face and a gentle contentment. They may have no drive to get to the top of their career, but they can be at peace and be happy.

That thirst for success, to have power over people's lives, to have money to buy anything you want. Can that ever be healthy? I believe that thirst for power is unhealthy and stems from feelings of low self worth.

So then, what is the impact of these narcissist leaders? If they are not altruistic, then they are totally self serving.

I believe narcissists are drawn to two things - money and power.

Some want money some want power, some want both. How many politicians and business leaders really want the people they have totally influence over to be happy? How many are totally selfless, only wishing for the happiness of those they serve?

In Marks and Spencer they design the layout of the stores to the maximum benefit of the customer, ie, lots of artificial light, music that gets people to buy more, access to suit the shoppers. No adaptations for the staff, who are on their feet for long shifts sometimes lasting 10-12 hours. The focus is always on where the money comes from.

Altruism, selflessness, compassion and care, those are things narcissist leaders simply don't have and as a consequence in society is quickly diminishing.

How much empathy do the managers of Marks and Spencer have for their staff, if they allow them to be on their feet all day with little natural light listening to the same music over and over again. It is always about the money. Always.

I have been thinking about going into politics, but I constantly question my real motivation behind that. I will be honest with you, it is to feel important and to have power. Yes I want to make life better for people, but there is a deep cynicism in me. My cause would be to improve mental health, to make therapy free to all. That people who have nowhere to turn, when they are in pain can seek the help they need to ensure they don't fall into that trap of numbness where you turn to drink and drugs. That you can get the help you need to find happiness again.

I am not sure if I am a narcissist or an altruist to be honest, maybe in time that will become clearer. But what I am sure of is that the government is failing to change a cyclical system.

Those children who are abused, become parents who are abusive. When can that cycle really stop, without free access to therapy.

All those generations, all those generations of pain, neglect and abuse that recycled themselves. The neglectful parents creating children who become neglectful parents. Emotionally detached - those who feel nothing creating children who feel nothing.

All that sadness, all that lack of trust, bad parents make bad parents and partners, love creates love.

10 SLEEPING BEAUTY

There is this disparity between who we really are, and who we present to the world. The one being the real self, the other being the protected self, a version we have formed based on the defences we have built to protect the true self.

The conditions of worth placed on us as children, the things we believe we have to do to feel accepted or loved. The experiences that make us feel ugly and unworthy. They sit inside us, and come out in the person we present to the world.

To use an analogy, the castle in sleeping beauty where for 100 years the thorny branches grow strong and thick to protect the princess from the real world, they grow thicker as time passes. We are inside the castle, and depending on when that happened and for how long will depend on how thick and strong that wall of weeds is around us.

Our defences are the thorns. Our true self is the princess, hiding frozen in time.

Put simply – some peoples defences are thicker and more ingrained than others. They have been there a lot longer, they are wrapped around and stuck to the true self.

If as a child the true self was rejected, abused or neglected in those early formative years when the true self was growing, the weeds will be very thick.

I believe only a very deep and profound attack on the true self would allow those individuals to reach self reflection – looking inwards, instead of outwards. Where healing can begin to take place, where real feelings of anger, sadness and joy can finally be felt.

My pain, my defences, grew over a shortish period from the age of 30 until 38. But I can still detect them, suffocating me, stopping me from feeling. Stopping me from feeling empathy for me, meaning I am then unable to feel empathy for another.

My husband, had a much bigger task at hand, so I do not hate, and for those 8 years while I tried to break down his defences with love, I could never do it. Only he can break down his own defences.

I reached a point at which I could not carry on, and looking back to use the analogy of the frog again in the pot of boiling water, I wish I had jumped out sooner.

This is why I think we need to allow our children to be free, to let their conscious lead them, not for us to control but guide. To encourage their own empathic responses, allowing them to build that gut instinct. That gut instinct which I lost during my emotionally abusive relationship with the covert narcissist.

I believe that is essential for the future, so that they don't need to keep asking advice, like I did, when I found myself in a confusing and emotional abusive period of my life, where I didn't have the answers and could not interpret what I saw with certainty.

This was supposed to be a book about narcissists. But I have come to realise that narcissism is simply a detachment from ones own feelings, or one's true self.

Narcissists, those that have detached from their feelings at some point in their life often try to control those in their lives which is why they then often come to abuse those closest to them. They feel out of control so they try to control those around them.

Power and control is such an important part of abusive relationships. If one person in the relationship has suffered a trauma, loss, neglect or abuse in the past, and detached from their feelings, they will not be able to handle any kind of change or feeling vulnerable in the relationship so will do everything they can to control that person so they don't have to feel vulnerable and "out of control".

They remember that feeling of being out of control, and to go back there is worse than death. Those who are not narcissists, those with healthy integrated feelings, who are connected with their "self" can't easily understand this. It is difficult to.

I feel I have seen both sides, which is why I want to share my story. I have felt detached from my feelings and numb, and I have felt very much aware of my feelings too.

A narcissist is not going to easily go back in time to a point when they were totally out of control and at the mercy of an abusive other. If they didn't kill themselves then they some how had to function, had to find a way to carry on with life. But that meant no longer being vulnerable, but being in control.

To not feel the feelings of pain anymore, but then at the same time not feeling those of joy either. To feel real true love you have to risk getting hurt, but narcissists can't feel the pain of loss, or the pleasure of joy.

For a narcissist to get back to feelings is to remember that time, when they nearly died. It is that feeling I had. I can only describe it as a wave coming over me, and knocking me off my feet and I just couldn't grab on to anything and stay standing up.

It is agony. Which is why you will find true narcissists won't seek therapy, they have found a way to function that works for them, it is the only way that works for them. To go back over those painful memories, would be like reliving that torment, that torture all over again. Yet if they don't revisit that trauma and integrate those feelings, i.e. feel them – scream, shout and cry, where rage wells up, where the deepest sorrow comes over you. Where you lose control and you can't hold on to anything, but there in the dark, if they can search and look and feel there will be a tiny spark. Then all of a sudden inside of you, there is a tiny spark. Hidden in the shadows, behind all that pain, and all those walls built to protect ones vulnerability there will be a tiny light of hope.

Like an ember – and with a mental health professional help that tiny spark of light can grow. As those feelings very slowly and painfully start to rise up again inside of you. But this needs to be done steadily in a controlled manner with a professional who understands this process. And it will feel awful for a long time, until then suddenly it gets easier.

This is how I would see a narcissist getting help and changing. But they have to see the issues, and they have to want and desire the change.

Therapy only works if the client wants to go, if the client has a goal to work with. When I went to therapy it was so painful to bring all these feelings up, that once a week didn't seem enough and when I wasn't in therapy I wanted to drink more than I had before.

It was very interesting, I would feel very depressed for a day, really dark. But then the next day I would feel fantastic. I think that was a very natural progression of the reawakening of those feelings that had been turned off. To allow the rage in, and the sorrow, would later lead to me allowing in the joy too. You can only disconnect from other people's pain (i.e. not care when you hurt someone) if you are disconnected from your own pain. If you cannot feel your own pain, you cannot feel anothers.

The purpose of this book was to pass on what I have learnt, but that is easier said than done. When you have been desperately unhappy for 7 years, and then come out the other end with such strength and clarity. You want to share the happiness, the solutions. But I know its not that easy.

I read and researched narcissists and then read some more, and went on more support forums online than you would believe. This I suppose was like group therapy, people that were feeling the same things as me. Taking bits of what helped them and adapting it to my situation. I was also able to get free therapy through a charity for 6 weeks.

In time over two years, I got stronger, things became clearer and I became happier. But more than anything I felt in control. I no longer needed to ask advice like I used to from close family and friends. Counselling, or therapy is about making ourselves stronger, basically growing in confidence about what we think we should do. About who we are, and what decisions to make without relying on anyone else. It is finding ourselves, whoever we are and knowing what is the right decision for us. Basically after a while I knew what to do, I didn't need to ask anyone anymore.

All I can hope is that my story will help one person, that's my only desire. As I spent many years being unhappy, and that feels like such a terrible waste.

That is such a regret for me, but writing my story, in a way stops me feeling those regrets. Because if my story and my situation and how I got out of it, helps others, then those years were not a waste. They do have a purpose.

But what I feel, and the experiences I have had and the strength I have found inside, is very much my story and my situation. I hope it is helpful. I think it will be but everyone has had a different "ride" when it comes to narcissistic abuse.

When it comes to narcissists, or as I prefer to call them "those detached from themselves" there are many different types. It all depends on when this detachment occurred, ie when did their trauma take place and for how long. Was it the death of a parent when they were young? Or a mother that provided all of their physical needs but none of their emotional ones. Or were they sexually abused as a toddler, before the age of awareness.

There are so many awful things that can happen to people, where they feel out of control. If this trauma happens over a long period, then maybe there is less hope that this person can change.

But that is not my job, to make an assessment on hope, in whatever situation you find yourself in. Or whatever narcissists you encounter in your life, be that a boss, a friend, a parent, a husband or wife. Everyone's story is different. Giving up hope for me, was the greatest release and the most important step for me to find a future again. But everyone is different, this is only my story.

The most important thing to remember with any narcissist, is that you can't change them. Only they can change themselves and this involves introspection, something that they struggle with. So if they can't self-reflect on their behaviour, and they can't empathise with the pain they are causing their loved ones. And they can't then try to address that with a professional, then you know there is no hope.

That person, that narcissist has to see it themselves. Even if they do get a glimpse of their true reflection I find it is only fleeting, ie it doesn't seem to be sustained. For to go to that part of themselves that they find so abhorrent, that place where they feel immense guilt and shame, is such a painful and awful place for them to go. So even if they go there once for a few seconds, it will take a lot of effort for them to go back there again. And the question is why would they go there? To such a painful place.

I think the answer to this is if they really feel they have something to lose. It would have to be something massive, a huge loss for them for it to be worth dredging all that pain up again. Coping mechanisms, such as going numb, or alcoholism, drug or sex addiction, gambling. They help us to cope, they help us to survive. They cover a pain hidden deep inside, but to uncover that pain needs insight and a mental health professional guiding one back to those traumas in a safe and trusting way.

In a marriage when you are suffering on a daily basis and you threaten to leave as the situation is so awful, living with a narcissist. You wonder why that doesn't motivate them enough to self reflect, to empathise and seek change. But I think we all underestimate how entrenched narcissist can be.

Some narcissists may feel different and on the edge of society, looking at everyone else and not feeling quite as "normal". But that is not enough to motivate change. Even when everyone around them is crying and screaming and abandoning them left right and centre. (often in intimate relationships rather than in the work place) They are not really affected by any of that, they don't really care, so again have no reason to seek change.

They always say it is the other person who is to blame, the other person is at fault. They never look within, because that risks their very being, their very existence, to feel shame or guilt is not an emotion they can allow in.

Every situation is different and all I can do is tell my story. From my perspective, the non physical – i.e. the verbal and emotional abuse from a narcissist is not something that people really talk about. And I was not hit on the outside, you won't see any bruises on my body or face. But look inside and there are many – well it has changed me fundamentally as I have described I now feel like a narcissist.

I believe these relationships with narcissists where the abuse is non physical is happening every where, all the time, in many marriages and between many parents and children.

Many families where every day is a struggle, where there is someone deeply unhappy making life hell for everyone else. These people are always right, these people never say sorry, and they don't seem to be able to care about how others are feeling. That is your typical narcissist and this is my story which I think is a very common one.

But like I said at the beginning, writing this has been a very useful journey for me and I want so desperately for other people to see things with such clarity. But for me it was a long process, and while I feel so good now and so clear. It takes time, and you have to work through confusion and anger, and sadness.

What I have learnt may be different to what you will learn, I just hope it helps in some small way. Even over writing this book, maybe I have let in a bit of hope. But that is the hope that I will change, not that I can change another.

It is accepted that we have unconditional love for our children, but not for our husbands or wives if they are abusive, there always comes a point when you walk away. Even if you can see the pain in their past, if they are hurting you and don't seek help it's accepted that the only option available is to walk away. This protects you and your children.

Perhaps there are some people with spiritual or religious beliefs who believe that they should show their husband or wife unconditional love. I don't know what you the reader believes.

I believe in forgiveness, and to let our hearts be flooded with love and compassion. Some people might choose to stay in these marriages. That is not my decision to make.

I still care for my ex husband Simon. I suppose I can see the soul within. Yes I still love him in a way but I do not want to stay around for the abuse. Will this person ever look at themselves and risk self-reflection and change, I don't think so, not in my situation.

In time I have begun to see that to self reflect is to risk their very existence, and I wouldn't expect or ask them to do that. For theirs is a lonely world and that is punishment enough surely. Where true love and genuine long lasting intimacy is absent.

So I don't seek punishment or retribution staring at their own reflection and believing it is perfect is not a happy place to be. Where they can only see their reflection and never the depth and beauty of trust, commitment and intimacy.

CPSIA information can be obtained
at www.ICGtesting.com
Printed in the USA
LVHW091755030821
694341LV00007B/1198

9 781521 332085